Where Bodies Again Recline

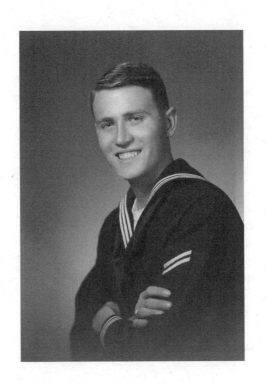

Also by Harry E. Northup

Books
Amarillo Born
the jon voight poems
Eros Ash
Enough the Great Running Chapel
the images we possess kill the capturing
The Ragged Vertical
Reunions
Greatest Hits: 1966-2001
Red Snow Fence

Audio
Personal Crime
Homes

Where Bodies Again Recline

Poems

Harry E. Northup

To FRANK BOYER
10-7-11
BEST REGARDS
Harry E. Northup

cahuenga
PRESS

Acknowledgments

Some of these poems have appeared in
Chiron Review, Askew & The Nervous Breakdown.

Copyright 2011 by Harry E. Northup
ISBN: 978-0-9715519-9-2
Library of Congress Control Number: 2010916110

Cover art: Olivia Sanchez-Brown
Front cover & back cover photos: Larry Nelson
Book design & typesetting: Ellison / Goodreau
Printed by McNaughton & Gunn, Inc., Saline, MI

Cahuenga Press is owned, financed and operated by its poet-members James Cushing, Phoebe MacAdams, Harry E. Northup, and Holly Prado Northup. Our common goal is to create fine books of poetry by poets whose work we admire and respect; to make poetry actual in the world in ways which honor both individual creative freedom and cooperative support.

Cahuenga Press
1256 N. Mariposa Avenue
Los Angeles, CA 90029
cahuengapress.com

Contents

Where Bodies Again Recline   11-2-04 to 8-7-07

lincoln highway | 16
green meadow foreground born | 18
mother forgiveness | 20
single round light in black night | 21
& we all fall upwards | 23
feminine | 25
where bodies again recline | 27
gifts | 29

White Bird Above Fire   2-6-08 to 9-3-08

White Bird Above Fire

heart follows | 36
white swan wings open above | 38
stillness, golden boat like a shoe | 40
red in its entirety: end | 42
arm light crooked support | 44
blue light dark leaves | 46
single white bird above fire | 48
porch where she stood | 50
candles like red soldiers | 52
golden eternal ship into water | 54
wind above house | 56
half the world away | 58
bird beak top hat white arrow | 60
what was lost, gained | 62
to distinguish love | 64
she opens she waves he waves | 66
figure, human length, rises | 68
web with trumpet & green leaf | 70
like a breeze the final caress | 72

Blue Final

wish upon a star: blood awning | 76
blue final | 78
brother's love reassures | 80
sunflowers then & now | 82
bends head in remembrance | 84
bees around dark interior | 86
night before birth | 88
brother's harmony | 90

Fire Bones   9-4-08 to 1-25-09

Fire Bones

moon & winds | 96
shadows silenced: talk back | 97
early morning news | 99
green leaves' dam | 101
weather vane: crossed arrows | 103
solace remembered | 105
before sleep | 107
fire bones | 108
skins | 110
golden belt around her waist | 111
white arrows surround center | 113
zeus in a hurry: eye within leaves | 115
whale juxtaposed with golden light | 117
friendships in market | 119
black vertebrae encased in golden light | 121
heart no longer lost | 123
golden lamps around the tips | 125
fingers open eyelid's heart | 127

Circles Where The Waters Meet

arrows' yellow bonnet | 130
circles where the waters meet | 132
golden arrows, eye, bull | 134
santa ana winds like oceans | 136
need has meaning | 138
above the blue mountain | 140
fires from horses & arrows shooting | 142
sunflower's concentric circle: escapes | 144
bench, rain, night, sun | 146
sunflower eye with green wings | 148
golden cradle | 150
saxophone on side like life raft | 152
wings & hand, stars beyond | 154

For Holly Prado Northup

Where Bodies Again Recline

(A Long Poem Composed from

11-2-04 to 1-25-09)

Where Bodies Again Recline

11-2-04 to 8-7-07

lincoln highway

"my wild irish rose
the sweetest flower that grows
you can search everywhere
but none can compare
with my wild irish rose"
my mother's favorite song
along with "easter parade"

she wrote me letters
& i saved 209 pages
from 1966 till 1970, when she died
she ended letters with
"please excuse the mistakes
all my love, mother"

lincoln highway, the coast
to coast highway, gather her
children
gather georgie from virginia,
her firstborn, the hero, the
chief radioman, fbi agent
gather bobbie, her second born,
the presbyterian minister,
missionary, the straight a
student
gather dorothy from her farm
in ohio, dorothy with her white
teeth & joyful smile, a beauty queen,
housewife, mother & church worker
dorothy, who memorized a sermon
she wrote, who waited for the

sunday when the minister got sick
dorothy, who gave her sermon
gather jim, who was & is a big
success, who is like daddy & has
mother's heart
gather harry from east holly-
wood, who is like his mother
in heart & worry

gather sunday mid-day dinners,
roast beef & mashed potatoes & gravy,
fried chicken
gather hard work & family,
ironing board & washtub
gather flower-printed dresses
in the closet
gather work all day at the post
office, drive 12 miles home,
cook dinner, do dishes, iron
clothes
gather driving 12 miles to the
fox theater, gather driving the
lincoln highway with george e.
& jim & harry
in the panhandle of misery lost
"you had a good mother, harry,
you're a lot like her," margaret,
georgie's wife, said

                                    11 2 04

green meadow foreground born

the golden & brown bricks
& the horses with chariots around
an eye like a saïl at sea
the golden, jagged arrow down, flames

cross at the middle of each
circles upward, leaves golden
my love an arrow & a heart
a long golden arrow upward into

the blue – golden arrow dispatched
from golden plant waving
hands circle unto red flames dancing
outrageous planes, circles

red flags follow a plane
circular as a wanting heart
finally, the bright golden road
determines solace no longer, denies

brotherhood absent, for the black
surrounding wrappings do not enclose
the blue & red heart deep but vivid
a place to rest, to sit – all day has

the time been warm – a train by the bed
magenta, aqua, scarlet folds upon folds
door, tree, praying mantis, deep dark-
ness, stars – breath thin like an aqua

membrane, deserted street with violet
shovel, wide as the street, high as
the one story buildings, the opened
scarlet heart closes, the hands again

like fragile beige leaves
cows, horses, legs like bottoms of sofas
& earth grows underneath
house top, light, forward rushing

all the trees white
& the fall forever more, an undecided
loss, streak of lightning upward
chandeliers of light, one descends

light gone, but the arrow, hands alight
a plant with red flower aslant in
golden bowl – the light across horizon
towards darkened house – the house

covered with leaves to its chimney
golden arrow down, an acorn with light
streams upward – a bright green
movement across the frame & rushes

like water as a hammer strikes, rings
light shoots up in circular movements
births, a cross with blue-lavender flow-
ers – waterfalls, forms skin around whale

1 30 06

mother forgiveness

how i have been loved
loved by risen sabres, by violent
forgiveness
by quiet faraway losses
loved by a tender mother's son
whose thoughtfulness surrounds
the damaged building hurt & now
lighter colored stones

"the japanese foot bridge," "the
cattle wallow" – monet & catlin
brothered by lion's biting vulnerable
neck

in absences of brotherhood
man has no image
love has risen with gifts & laughter
clean, thrifty, chosen journey

his sister's handwriting persistently
clean – no lonely death, no silence
the strict emotion cannot willingly
turn around

he has to sit next to his wife of 63 years
he describes udon & then tempura
the middle 3 couples sailed together
laughed over the black queen
clean, tender, absent night

10 5 06

single round light in black night

yellow sunflower tips its head
to be near a banana yellow flower
sun twinkles, a chain of bright sun
stars lead down into royal blue lake

where many more form a single path
plane outward rush in dark sky – the
plane's jet exhaust fiery blue in night
golden arrow white frilly flower

near its tip – bright sun flies like
a plane – golden liquid poured into sun
sun in rear view mirror – double suns
fly up like space ship – short golden

arrow hits sun – when all of a sudden
sparks fly & the sun turns into a
rectangle & then transforms into a
magenta horizon – moves above the

whole earth – single light arises
climbs the sky – now dark blue
moon blue & blue liquid is being
poured – darkness surrounds us

old things, mountains, statues, being tossed
sun far out, with flower-like fringe
woman's face, blue eyes, finger,
hand, wooden cross – behold cylindrical
column barely faint its emerg-

ence – crown, white-cupped flower
gray cat sits, white arrow, turning circles
like tunnel surrounding a red candle
with flame – black roundness at horizon

dark clouds above blue eyes, figure thin
like a wisp, with white skull-like head
flowery, thin, watery arms, many arms
row a piano keys at angle, white blotchy

flower, hands down, covering part of statue's
bronze head – hands of a castle reach out
purple flowers cover night portion
the crown, laurel, first horizontal, then

turned on its side – golden church pipes,
in triangular fan, branch up – like corn,
like large grasshoppers sitting, waiting
golden pipes with scarlet bottoms

surround wholeness – golden wisps, like
smoke, curl at bottom & sweep upward
arrows up out of the wide golden bowl
arrows like jets fill whole bottom center

shoot out & magnificently the bottom
reverses deep & the missiled arrows
seem smaller & deeper away – huge
sunflower, like an ocean, with its dense
center brown seeds, its golden petals fires
dancing – blue splashes up white around

11 7 06

& we all fall upwards

the wings are white
& are petals of a sunflower
a white hand holds an arrow
lily opens, waterfall rushes

into its center a ring of fire
sustains itself in royal darkness
the men were proud of their humanity
kind women stood close, talked directly

white flag on arrow aslant
as a man played piano
golden wrappings around right forearm
center burst light

window flames, panels of hostages
center gold, lit candle, rocket retreats
coiled silver sharp wire
silver-frayed wings going upward

arrows downward, a man with raised
spear, gold beard, face hidden
he sweeps the world with his fire
a spear thrown into the dark sky

bursts into circular bright waterfall
washington monument length rectangle
the edges of a book, a huge white
still building like paint in an abstract

expressionist painting full of fury
in its stillness – sweeping wings
upward, all around the perimeter
the center full of arrows rushing

commuters in a row of blood, elevated
trains above, white lights like leaves
waving, entering a window
scrim, veil, scarlet in its homecoming

a curling honeycomb around a lit candle
an eye – the light shoots upward
into the darkness – an animal cry
like a siren – lavender shirt buttoned

blood appears & the shirt recedes into
redness, dissolves – emotional as the
cold earth – the tops of trees in
morning light: sunflower & cornets

man falls from a mountain & swoops
a golden surfboard breaks vertigo
single golden leaf, uprooted tree
golden knife into tree, trapeze

into sky – light-silver-capped mountain-
tops, black wings above – green bursts
the white solid rectangle again
emotion fills the heart, white wings,
black wings, testimonies: red-leaved
wings falling: gold almost touches gold
the moon pours down its misty absence

                              12 15 06

feminine

the curved white lines rain down
morality questioned, materialism
heralded, vanity queened, delicious
bewilderment walks east on sunset

forever saddened – half a cross
what has no heroine? greed
hungers for land & calls it honor
loses the gift & names all from one

business town, credit rating files
away, reduces itself to refrain:
thee & only thine flies holy silver
where then is the only golden

connected road vertical & horizontal
the black ship barely seen against
the royal blue night cleans itself
against the descent always to be last

darkened, not entirely cleaned
she rises with all silver 16 inch
guns blazing & the angel flies above
a golden chicken finds solace in

the center – ships at sea torn &
rustled in searoar – god save the
floating, large, mint-green hat
honor, trust, spirit, compassion

from home lost to house to mine
above all to my corrections to
my powerful lusty golden fire bolt
striking both ways in the ferocious

sky – forms a single-seemingly
limitless arrowhead fired by a black
dormant & deadly sea, its winged
waves parted sending raised winged

waves left & right, an upswoop till
clouds golden bestow broken vanity
rest from constant muse, to reassure
a turning, golden rings, around a

cylinder: my house, my name, a lost,
large, empty red shoe – high as a house
whose heart, with cliffs like big sur,
curves around a darkened bay

a hand with a ring, a lost earring
what drives a golden car to shore up
against the rising credit: solace in a
false grace, accumulated sorrowful

flowers unleashed beside a tall green
tree with golden rings, sparkling red
lights: heart & golden birds surrounding
my arms, a golden hand extends into blue-
ness

1 2 07

26

where bodies again recline

in the primacy of law, the bootleg
version, there will be no superiority
of money, of celebrityhood, of
loss, lack, ignorance, rigidity, simple
down home rootedness

there will be listening to one another
a recognition of brotherhood, a will-
ingness to see past vertical mobility
there will be family, love, rosy cheeks
white teeth of love, blushing
no gender skin loss wall – wanting
let's go

friendship, simple as stone, as water,
as here, what's in my pocket is what
i place on the table
where the visiting team is the home
team
where the son treats his brother
like his mother treated him

where glorious is not vanity
where brother does not fly past
brother to go to another land
where competition actually has
a heart of compassion
where the airport is not a home
but a place to go inward from

where bareness, simplicity, honesty
are virtues – where godness, god-
head, bones, skin, heart bend
into wind, into rockies, golden wheat
doors open
not only in small town day time

but night time of dark souls
of all lostness, all humility
simply crisp night air, simply
round moon, no fires, tall palm
trees, quiet jubilees, quiet
families eating dinner – be still
in the quiet wind
after the burning

5 13 07

gifts

highway 30 ten miles
left, curve up & over the viaduct
sod house gone, newly graded field
brownson grade school where i played
soccer, cut my finger, recited
"o captain! my captain!" where 4
lambs & 1 goat greeted my return
where i got a's in english, d's in
deportment, warmed my winter body
the units gone to jungle, a few
blue collar workers live in the
few habitable concrete units

shelter shelter – it's not even
a brother's love
it's a wife's love, a cat pawing
for dawn pets behind the ears

to live in the movies
to start a fire in a wheat field
at age 5, to describe the arsonist
exactly like me, wearing a sailor
suit

"i have a vivid memory of looking
out my window, mid-morning, summer,
& seeing harry walking
with a baseball bat over his shoulder
& he's carrying a baseball glove"

isaac martinez was a great left-
handed hitter, batted third, played
left field & first base, led the team
in rbi's, inner strength, quiet, of
the earth – 50 years later we met
& we were respectful to each other

isaac, ike, rudy, lola – depot
friends of the 1950s
& the depot's closed for forty years
& it's this age that tells me there
is a rise & a fall & yet we are
still memories of each other's youth

& my friend conrad dead, & ferdinand
dead, & mrs. hernandez dead
my mother & dad dead & my brother
& i visited their grave site, he
bought flowers; i said, "thank you,
mother & daddy, for the life you
gave us; we came from a good
family" & there were flowers
on 2/3rds of the graves in
greenwood cemetery, east of sidney
it rained as it always does for a
funeral – careers die, youth dies,
trust dies, money decays brotherhood

all holiness must die & be reborn
in new roads, new rain, – memory
remains blackness itself
memory strengthens kindness

a photo of a young sailor in san diego
returned 50 years later to an old
actor in sidney, nebraska
a yearbook of photos of a high school
actor, athlete, orator, kept by an older,
pretty, mexican lady, rescued, kept,
returned to a man returning to his
boyhood dance 50 years later

blackberries, lodgepole creek, viaduct,
fights, love, respect, loyalty, friendships
hallowed is the hearth of nebraska!
hallowed my father's work, my
mother's heart, a surprising friend's
remembrance: wheat & fire

8 7 07

White Bird Above Fire

2-6-08 to 9-3-08

White Bird Above Fire

heart follows

waterfalls onto white crown
white airplane precedes lengthy white
serpent, returns, upturns
playfully – so short, cannot deny

for whomsoever matures must be
vulnerable, arms furiously blurred
leaf-like arrow broken into many
small arrowhead images sparkling

she appears in mint-green, waves
blueberries spill out of white crown
defend not loss, accept sadness, dismay
thou has lost thy brother, thy first

family, not killed, the large white bird
grounded, though white circles turn
vertically nearby, & a man strums a
banjo – the two furthest figures sit

like lincoln in memorial, trained white
falcon with black eyes, tombstones trail
up hill, no eyes, white brilliant clouds
front blueness – my sister's eyes

like a peach, like a bag of groceries
with leaf like a scythe – white
figure with upturned white wings
band of gold around her waist

city glows gold fronted by cacti
ears of corn bright as coal in green
sheathes – bags full each with stick
in center reveals far off still blue

single white cloud like a lagoon
domesticity broken by river low
propeller heart – arrows slam into
black granite – one single arrow zips

city glows, golden strings tied like
a gift – then all a hand, a rushing
westward, its flame eastward, golden
bridge – top blackness crumbles

specify linkage golden heart
specify heart lost furrows
a red crown, hearth, red car, road
the road has been traveled, enduring
ravishing, cardinal, burnt heart

2 6 08

white swan wings open above

filings pulled by a magnet fill
the sky like locusts while a single
slant of light located horizontally
the name bracketed by apostrophes

remains a circumference around the
earth – stalks jet from lower right
to top center, thick arms – fists meet
an opened hand falls back, friendship

based on here, what now, blood, will
openness alone wait willingly, be a
virtue, dark wings carry gold, a flash
of crumbled light blooms up past

flower tips, black shield hides heart
a road long & hilly, clouds puffs of
explosions, the beams shoot singularly
high into the black sky, keep opening

wings, while open an opposite incoming
light hits the center – a ship
alight, held in the palm, carnage
of old, golden, precisely elegant

the race began, sparkles green,
red, rhubarb red, the enfolding leg
& in the hills, explosions, knives
wash ashore like spines ever last-

ing a golden path like lava going
outward, airplane blue, ship like
dawn, ship's bow pushed upward
wide beach fresh foam clean half

circle, two tears drop – sails down
bare black branches – ship washed
not ashore but unto other boats,
boats pile atop boats stacked up on

black rocks, a single golden light atop,
above two wings in primary blueness
& wrecks, water rushes the bottoms
her face, one eye, sensual, half-seen

above, behind, to the side, a cloud
passes above her eye, outward heart
escapes, desires, connects, she alone
a constant will not waver, bends
opens whiteness, remains heart, arrives

3 4 08

movie Shots

stillness, golden boat like a shoe

the gila monster wears a head-
dress of red arrows
white sails, golden moon path on
water's arrival
hawk flies sideways, one long white

wing touches earth
legs of light
path slowly river mounds
cactus strong like bowed knife
shoeless lady – fire beneath her

the blue has a tinge of red
under it – defend her
from quiet street & leaves inside
the house – the long arrows are
silently stacked

her skirt sways, pitchforks cross,
upstairs fences slam down
white wing on shoulder in dark
the turning upside down table
her white dress moves upward

trap her deceit! the long leaves
sprout out & upward like rockets
she turns, dazzling light, a drill
fires beyond – flames like chorus
girls' legs – unison & bright

the long worm turning around
a skull – bright feathered arrows
in a row on a hill up the feet up
the legs, daggers wearing top hats
dance around fire – feathers now

one has wings & many are wrapped
in light linen, a vase with fires
shaped like splendid daffodil tips
ripped, shaded, branches flags of
nations circle, sideways burning

as they tip, all like birds with mouths
open, upright, wanting fire moon-
light path warm arms – quiet hall
sunlight on green leaves
the whitest light down the tree

streaks across the upcoming arrow
her eye dark blue-gray emerges
blue waters, circles of golden light
leaves of golden light down blue river

5 29 08

red in its entirety: end

star with mint-green interior lines
white-gold lights surround & sparkle
white wings, like crescent moon,
swoop sideways, playfully, quickly
dive & surround like open cup

honesty hurtful open – surrounds
& dances: small white rings
long jade arrowhead – leaves lengthen
gold burnishes – should repent should
forgive – earth land moves outward

blossoms, keeps reaching & circles
again darkness – but golden tips
ascend, star wider, more golden
hammock made of gold, leaves, trees
finally a horse at top left edge

of planet – its body shields darkness
rockets explode upward in all directions
golden arrows golden hand
multiple arrows like waves receding
cloud forms large face profile

arrows buzz left to right, right
to left, face moves right to left
arrows downward like schools of
fish zip & quiet & up into waterfall
origin: her naked body behind

waters sweep upward, like fish
downward like surfers down high
wave – calm blue at bottom, spiky
large fish moves slowly, ghostly
one arrow stirs makes bracelet

golden legs dance, petals blossom
arrows upward like petals of
sunflower: mercy, fires in
basket, sideways by her waist
as she walks – we home – hand

spills ripe bing cherries on table
thistle green anger deceased
sadness lost – arrows speed like
boats outward seeking heights
in quietness – two angle toward

in the quiet

each other – two mint-green eyes
downward sweeping lights surfing
a plane at bottom – arrows shoot
up, blueness, long boats forgiving
peace, golden, long, serene fin

6 19 08

43

arm light crooked support

short electric lights fill the
front of a face – arrows form
perimeter fire like a crown
suddenly pulled, a cane formed
where has heaven sent me?

crawling on a branch, bridge
sprouts bright yellow flowers
sunflower with arrow stuck in
its heart – bright lights outward
long light path, bolt into sky

still be, quiet like a frog, telephone
pole, plane in far roar, two jeweled
eyes of cat – arrows' lights shoot
out in all directions – why shield?
for sheaves of wheat in hands

one powerful fiery arrow fills
sky, then it's all dark until spoils
of light tie ropes around wrists
one fire path at foot of mountains
shield, leaf whose heart sweeps

down like surfers, skiers, & onrushing
circular waters: clean breath
underneath clouds the bright length-
ening matches – turn downward,
turn into thousands of arrows

released, rolls over the world, a
single gold fish at center – with
constant revolving arrows in blue sky
crown gold & often wreath-like
two faces, in profile, kiss: tragedy &

comedy absent – the crown has opened
up a great ocean voyage – but fire
remains backward, sides perimeter
light above, open-mouthed crocodile
below – feet, hands, stars, deny heart

& our hands are full of golden wood
fires in circles on blue water & one
fire in center – arrows swoop into
ears large as malls, white-golden hair
races back, golden stalks like prairie
wheat, an eye behind swirls, seen & gone

6 26 08

blue light dark leaves

prayer hands at forehead
silver cross & black bear emerge
the bear runs through water puddles
knee bone, thigh bone connects to

high flying jet plane, bone out
of whirl, golden feathers at arrows'
tips, ready, light catches gold
gathers before spine journey over

mountain – hand rises, open
surety, mournfully, arrows strike
like planes, like flowers blooming
yellows outward fill circumference

from out of the opening a serene
earth – splashing volcanic gold
hands cradle it back & forth
small fires, wings – canoes, surfers

up rush to the left – arrows up &
then a phalanx turning back
little planes of gold – winged angels
black night white stars – splashing

up & down, a washing, yellow birds
relentless, one tall tree, sparse
branches – chair & table, pole with
propeller at top – red wood like

legs open up left & right, a golden
eye in great crawling creature
arrow, branch, backbone – one-
cell circle – flowers with purple

tips bloom, hand offers, animals
listen, plane with golden exhaust
hands like brooms sweep earth
golden petals surround molten

black stone: hearts' envy, vanity
sweep sweep golden – oars row
feathers, arrows, planes – boats
swimming man at surface

golden hand spreads – planes fly
out of dark abyss, swirling black
vertical cylinder, my love, my heart,
golden race track: golden arrowhead
in blue: cow skull, open mouth, two
red horizontal lines above serenity

7 1 08

single white bird above fire

fires burning, crowns across the
sea – plane, with burning wing, flies
a star hoisted, props the plane,
cradles it – through all our arms,

we fail, we reach out, brother loves
himself, his present family more
than the one he came from, ego, vanity,
our singers perform the old ballads

refrains die, swift white birds, like
ice skaters, swoop & turn, our hearts
& emotions die daily – desires shoot up
from a golden crown, die, veils of

smoke from aged candles invite
romanticism, behold, no separation
what small blue in the sky
we elect parts of ourselves & deny

blessings; the golden city on an island
does not include our neighbor's vote
should he be less wealthy, less like our
desire – we measure hearts with ring

sizes – for often hearts are rubble
tornado tracks, oil wells rise between
her naked legs, table set with far-
off star sparkling – straight long

knives of light surround our descent
what was killed remains hidden – it
tears at freedom – columns fall,
tumble, & a long crescent, like

antlers, forms a cradle around the
blue light moon – shreds torn, reveal
red deer, youthful, birds & arrows
forever territory – torn white wings

float – assemble the disassembled
heart, history, forced love but not
forgotten, sunflower alone among
long guns, dark & foreboding, golden

headdress, indian chief & horse in fire
the golden leaves leap forward
deliver me, white bird, white house
forgive the ache, the one long sharp
arrow on fire, cross, field burning

7 2 08

porch where she stood

jade lake, grasshopper, black
bridge – white pyramid – all family
white propeller sings take me
home, i am home – hands embrace

long white smoke reclines, curves
yellow tail feather – boxcars & box-
cars of coal heading east – yellow
fan, smoke & fire – escape the fear

car seat with sun lines vertical &
horizontal, thousands of thin wind-
mills whitely visible faraway hills
reflectors ready for snow visibility

golden roads flow beside each other
tumble into circular bales of straw
golden feathers: sister's heart
mercy & tenderness – golden leaves

square golden tin among greenery
take me home yellow flowers
i am home buttercups yellow leaves
green & golden floors hold lostness

journey into glass smashes face,
does not break; cleanses, does
not sever – wind blows & cleans
green stems in horizontal holdings

road golden like a furious train
leaf & white light explosion, face:
her merciful love – out from blue-
green earth – saved by wheat

rushes whipping in winds, prairie
viaduct, sod house gone, wheat
the daffodils of my youth, home
small, dilapidated, heart warm

trees diagonal in sky, road dis-
appeared alongside highway 30
parallel to interstate – point of
rocks, hill like train engine, long

memory met, fires, like leaves in
darkness, runaway, sheer cut, schism,
denied, golden leaves upside down
from heaven, green arms, golden hand

7 7 08

candles like red soldiers

one eye in the blue mountain
light shines at 45 degree angle – it brightens
rays shine down from the eye's
outer corner – golden leaves float

golden water flows over falls
smoke rises up & out at right angle
white makes triangle – golden circle
rushes around – bird with crocodile mouth

opens its mouth & smoke comes out
white birds, wings open, on pedestal
white flower half dead – silver
flowers line upward diagonally

forks, fires, knives, guilt has over-
whelmed sadness – caused unnecessary
killing – expose everything, the
wife said – golden tracks in each

direction: 2 one way, 2 the other, sameness
regrets – large sunflower petals
golden circular floor on columns
shelves with white pots, small rockets

slanted, in repose, blue river fore-
ground, city behind, golden wings
in boxes, trumpets raised, played
like guns, shooting at a far center

one branch of white petals, her heart
honest & comforting – leaves open,
horizontal light shines east & west
turquoise sky, white clouds, red tree

stage lights pulled from the ceiling
white chandelier, white leaves open,
crown rises – roads white in four
directions – gold rage, circle of stars

two long golden roads: black beetle
moves slowly eastward, large mouth,
white teeth: sun rays, red dress,
long white legs: corridors, rose at

deep center, teeth, water, cliff, teeth
covering teeth: whiteness shining
golden hand reaches upward, circle
of fire, raft, triangle, speed connects
burning fire: hand, arm, gold, candles

7 8 08

golden eternal ship into water

green candle burning, white cross
walks like old man – gains trinkets,
goblets, white hat, white (multi) wings
transforms into slender body with

tiffany lamp – turns furiously, nest,
candle burns – many wine glasses
wings from neck like sunflower
petals, few picked, hand, crown

curved scythe, short golden arrows
church white bull with silver bells
around neck – horizontal cross shin-
ing – carried pilgrimage, flowers up

into tree, single tree with several
arrows as branches – golden branched
held cross – hand from green sleeve
into darkness except for faraway

stars, hand outward like a fork
white cow, head turns into alligator
many white walkways – spokes on
water – white leaves, with arrow

feathers, admits loss of greenery
pipe pouring golden lava down
surface diagonal slashes up, forms
elbow, continues slanting upward
long river, with slight crooked

journey inland – many tributaries
like hand, hand grabs, vase
with flowers falls, red blood in light
dark full tree – white stems, from

heaven downward, lavender petals
surrounded by earthly fires
winged, golden figure swoops, fills
blue sky – one golden butterfly

with singed wings – golden weapons
forgiven, forgotten for single
green leaf – boomerangs memory
golden branches golden leaves fly

like insects – green & silvery
rushes – single silver spear
arrows, in a line, with golden feathers
pilgrimage, bridge, foreseen, circle
knife, hand, redness, heart, hearth
bugles & blue paper & fire aloft

7 10 08

wind above house

golden wreath with two swords
crossed like railroad crossing sign
one pulled back & plunged into light bulb
fire at tip – sparkler, mint rose

yellow leaf beside it, gun, arrow,
flag of sun light seen from train
sheath of thin golden leaves, surren-
der, let rose's wings be, golden

wreath zips toward ending light
watching roads & drivers – rockets shoot
up diagonally opposite directions
golden leaf from tree exhaust extinct

marries golden rain, black pyramid
seen by one eye, her majesty
mint-blue curve around planet
golden leaf drags heaven

mountain, with its lightened spine,
like roaring jaguar, she stands,
in glory, surrounded by golden light
white wings, white wings above people

two white feathers bestride a nest
with white road from its bottom
an avalanche of wintry death
arranges memory: sun, rectangle

with downward ropes, lavender
forearm, scar tissue at left elbow
moon & cloud far distance, white
elephant small as pygmy with

white cow nearby – white wings, large
seen above – a wine glass, empty,
holds up green veins – tree, arm
vertical, horizontal, rolling gold

bottoms of trees: fires climbing
black train fills horizon, quiet & then
rush – arrow falls backward from
sheath – beige sky, fort at moun-

tain top with flags hurling in
front – horse, feather – horizon alive
with lines of light & scarlet, beside
her one black arrow, forearm, center

exploding light in all directions, golden
peaked house moves upward through
wind, horses, feather flag, dark train
golden arrow, red arrow, misty train

7 12 08

half the world away

"i loved you from the first
moment you touched me in the park"
white feather, small fires
head on arm

tree branch, softness, warmth
white wings, arrow upward, hand
on belly, hand on back, small fires
revolve in a circle

center golden ball: resolve
swoosh like skier down mountain
curve, wings, star, animal closeness
white cross, spears crisscrossed

rays of light down, fires hallelujah
golden wings shield, butterfly
waterfall wide, clean, bright day
path full of light spreads

water falls into fires, yellow
fires into darkness – far-off guns
remind us revolving world
pyramids, small, yanked from fires

circle, fire like large leaf, forever
discarded tire, canteen, hands
crossed, phone – thousands of
single, pyramid-shaped sails above

far waters – one single golden boat
& sail, furious revolutions: grace
gone – green leaf stands with
edges like guns shooting

golden streams high height, single
each, drop – waters rush under
many rusted ships' weight
arrows circle down, fires circle

up: golden feathers, golden balls
of fire – black ship between
brightness – winged head perseus
monstrous whale head, mouth

arrows flying, foamed water ashore
figure receives arrows, martyred
waterfalls, blue umbrella, headdress
of golden arrows, vertical, horizontal
fire crown, half-sun, leaves fall

7 18 08

bird beak top hat white arrow

flags folded & put into basket
yellow rope tied around it
path taken, rider & light & helmet
white wings on great plane upward

telephone with draped wings
golden darts thrown white light
winged figures flying curving
upside down – dark wings of

planet moving – hushed, mint-green
figure like statue of balzac
arrow & string pulled back
black planet bowls through light

faraway, half cantaloupe planet
receives shot arrows – winged
figure above blue whale, stars
in between – yellow roses float

golden boat drifts – light shines
on seat in water – arrows come
over the mountain & curve down
rockets shoot up from shore

like rays of the sun, conquering
hat with thin pyramid atop
clown face, fires north horizon
high waterfall falls through crown

simple brown rocking chair, blue
drape behind – swords, spears, slash
light searching dark – turning
golden leaves crown, builds light

in front of window, golden collar
thin flowers dark meadow, dog,
golden hand, bull, deaths & light
dark tree, pedestal steps, places

for running water – red steps up,
water, fish, explosions, hands
severed, reaching, flowers bloom
fish mouth opens – from out of the

rectangular bloom, a black ship
emerges – gold around its edges
puffs of smoke smoke – hand, golden
cuff, flower in back pocket, white wing

7 20 08

what was lost, gained

a circle of propellers, blueness
moves into the far umbrella of sky
& rotates with arrows behind like
a pyramid-shaped space ship

where we were sent to recover
thankfulness & well wishes, no longer
just i, but yellow flowers bundled,
following, single arrows follow one

by one into loins, red face awakes
deep greenery, forget anger, hurt,
blown out assumptions, little fiery
ships upward into extinction

small fires circle, her waist candles
burning – all lotuses dead – the far
off center has not held – presses
working in blue corridors, sadness

falls – yellow-tailed arrows like bones
sticking out of center – swoosh down-
ward, spiky tails, wheels: milton's
fire hand; blake's water wheel

flowers, plane flies down into center
the giant fire wheel continues
like a waterfall, replenished by
moons, desires off the blue into

mountain, water backward out of
bugles – lights shine down on
black beetle body, rowers rush rows
fires atop black building – fire

like gold our arms rushing to hold
great waters behind dam, hoover,
colorado feeds, owens feeds
once we were desert, our family

veils death, love surrounds the fail-
ing banks, the long arrows downward
into deep cavern – jets, insects,
triangles of matches – arrows, roads

all ways everlasting, revelations,
glory, earth, river – sky with golden
explosions – one turning diamond in
fire, body compressed, human-like,
with propellers, triangles turning
spinning out most of blackness, stars

7 21 08

to distinguish love

faucet with light bulb on top
pipe with two hands, worn place
the first letter of the alphabet
all in a row – an arrow – words

are gold in darkness – hands go up
clarinet rolled – long revolving pipe
disintegrates – two shields with inner
handles, lengths joined, leaf light

leaf long light like valley shining
arrows with golden feathers, arrows
with red feathers, ghost of water
through rocks – arm outward like

a path, golden leaves slanted up
with goblet in center, fires around
the valley's crown – marching, crawl-
ing, circus-like, flowers, horizontal,

inside flowers, like magician's
trick, continue popping out, green
light behind mountain, golden nest
around eye, serving pitcher, small

& regal, destiny, rushes, sharp saw
back & forth, golden ash trails
rainbow straight, not curved
small hands move left to right across

the sky, small fires valley bottom
arrogance distinguishes golden
ball moving upward seized by hands
arrows dumped out of large sheath

fall & shoot & explode in fire, catch
fire, leave warmth, sleep near
like small boats on great waves
smoke through revolving light

light curves up left from center
light curves up right, negotiates
nest upward, umbrellas on stilts
arrows attack purple dark cloud

golden path moves between
magenta leaves, golden flower
rain falls into its center, opens
further, arrows shoot into flames

7 26 08

she opens she waves he waves

the wheels began to move
a long pole with net twirled
two of them, like a windmill
drawing the blue wind in

like tweezers open like scissors
horizontal, the yellow propeller
spins, shield defending, protects
white wings, yellow with cinnamon

butterfly wings, up & down, before
enlarged takeoff, yellow exhaust
blue sky – her legs in red stockings
sunflower petals blown back

as center moves back with force
white cross church front largest
in town – long time ago – cross
flies like plane – yellow under

dark smoke at dusk, yellow flag
all across the wide waterfalls
curved explosions downward
smokestacks at sea, path behind

trees shine light en masse out-
ward, small boats in circle move
down toward center, we all fall
her face half mask, some merge

some still, the young grow, learn,
leave, in unison upward against
sea wave, circles of boats, surfers,
arrows, youthful pursuits, shining

lights around darkness at deep center
like flowers with blooms nodding, in-
ward, trumpets blare, strut, white
pearls mute openings – webs lift

light gains miles circumference
lifts, denies death as death denies
only from my inner death, love wings
dam high holds back, light down,

flares dawn, each succession, long
golden path with propeller, like vol-
canic ash down its side, webbed
mountain, leaves, blackness lightness

7 29 08

figure, human-length, rises

propeller, jet exhaust, man
running, eye like sunflower
center – blood moves above, a cross
flames on mountain side

blue eye with silver surrounding
man in snow's center, in eye's center
white road – hand reaches up
grabs branch – white flowers on

snow, leopard gains, world money
gold, the size of a car, shines
low waterfall feeds river

flowing east – white flowers
shoot out of sun – our host
rains, memory, lasting flowers
waters splash up, sunflower sways

golden gun, cocked, pointed
two multi-colored arrows rise
suit coats in closet, waters rain
down on blue swans, solace, seren-

ity, yellow flowers beside ring
gondola, our hearts stuck with flowers
large shield, many embedded arrows
deep center below greenery

sadness, hope, slow walk in forest
waterfalls: blue-white shoulder
regrets? no — live right now in
greenery, shield's loss, light sweeps

up: many jets, waterfalls width
enormous whiteness rushing
finally night, house on hill, stars
arrows revolving, arrows reversing

white door, flowers in darkness
arrows in sheath like umbrellas
golden figure, vertical, inside turning
red flags above, spears, arrows, petals

white light above many figures
heart, soul, words, real gold, sorrow
nowhere, death nowhere, nothingness
white light out of opened coffin
sprinkling gold dust, death joy

8 1 08

web with trumpet & green leaf

a golden bird spreads its wings
six necklaces round her neck
shields, surround, loss, kept, re-
mains, death decides, forgotten

finds, relief, heart hope journey
golden arrows, sun, eye – she has
our soul – white falling shapes
like cut cauliflower sections

red fire at back of rectangular
motion – white bird flies
world like movie screen, darkness
surrounds – small white fish

swim lengths & curves – shield
with hundreds of arrows embedded
white stream horizontal, whiteness
intersects at southern end

man's figure in prostration, purple
hole in back, sacred golden
winged arrows blare out backward
circles of light, chapel at center

circles dance, fall back, find
distance, balance, sorrow has
weight that rises & dies, leaves like
arrows form circle, encircled

journey home, light down, arrows
rush up opposite sides like washing
motion – the endless golden
arrows, demonic, deep, no solace

dark blue eye, still, large like
planet, under sunflower, dried out
beneath rainbow – friendship
surprises – figure flies up like

raised trumpet – golden wheat falls
in cylinder-like form, no external
wall, circle of grown trees: hori-
zontal swimming partners, chorus

beauties – surround – lake with
lights up: stairs to top row, night
nature – golden arrows curve up
off cliff in unison, home breath
shield, drum, skin, table, hands home

8 8 08

like a breeze the final caress
(for holly prado northup)

a white tornado spins, drops
rain, shines fire, wings with
knives sheathed, revolving bone
white tree – golden highway

a crown, nest revolving, upward
path shoots & two horizontal half-
circles meet, waterfall wings
tree-like motion spins

red grapes, clusters around golden
center, night with stan getz playing
"alfie," breeze, no high humidity,
"what a difference a few degrees
make"

golden cathedral: spinning top
lilacs, flowers trailing, flashlight
shining down – sunflower with
petals glowing up – arrows like

jets rush round the circumference
many sunflowers strewn from
shoulders, fires of them, golden
bach pipes – petals like fires rush

up sides of canyons, double in
height, waterfalls wide as ocean
recede in dawn's rosy light
propeller at center of valley

no shadow act nor arrows like
thistle – still face – arrows like
lightning – arrows shoot out in
a diagonal fashion, buddies in war

long white plane-like salamander
arrows, like flags, dance around
perimeter, fire glows at planet's
being eclipsed – peacock tail spread

in gold wheat fields lit from above
at night – dark path – arrows shoot
out from rectangle's center, one
golden ring around large black

bird's long neck – feathers dance
arrows transform into golden circle
bird flies upsidedown, below a
golden boat, golden twisting serpent
sunflower rushes forward, with rose's
fragile closing petals, arrow departs
like a breeze the final caress

8 10 08

Blue Final

wish upon a star: blood awning

white star, trampoline of light,
grace & kindness close darkness
a held cup speeds upward
circles blinding scorpion's tail

past warmth where beast had slept
sword in horizontal sheath within
light, its arrowhead revolves de-
tached like buddha: eternal sorrow

golden path encircles its reach
ladders fall – its two ends meet
at center: kitten face, owl,
crescent – golden fist's determi-

nation, baseball diamond seen from
above, heart in meadow, refrain:
memory with manners – golden
path goes beyond sportsmanship

great winged bird comes to meet,
light bulb, golden leaves, fire,
cut oval, curls into itself like a
rolled up sleeping bag – coins fall

on top of coins – the old sorrow
hungers, carries residuals, shows
5 figures around communal table
arrows, like rockets, shoot up

golden tree, lit saxophone, plane,
bird, dark tree, white envelope
drifts down, two eagles form circle
with their necks: shining light

spins, thrashes, washes up, water-
falls, freeways up hills, arrows
circle up, form nest, skyscraper
in darkness – golden net forms

large hammock, muted horn, tails
like gloves, glass with arrows tum-
bling – nest sideways on serpent's
back – long paths into single stars

triangle light, boat appears, daybreak
golden arrows shoot out of sheath
amongst the stars, tied white bow,
trumpets lined up, firing red lights
white bird, wings scroll sorrow dead

8 15 08

blue final

hawk flies, white propeller moves
like shark in blue waters, smooth
& turns quickly – long white wings
in wind's lit path – hurries home

white rose with necktie forgives
hands circle the face on sunflower
yellow flames outward – rushes
back & forth in wind – yellow lilies

tongues bend, cello stands in field
yellow leaves' tips – red & white
path strikes through, a reckoning
buttercups before doorways

sunflowers move like jellyfish
green leaves dark center – arrows
& feathers, homes & doors – flames
lengthen, make hands below paths

yellow arrows shoot up from sides
dark sky, rain, house top with half
moon missing – sunflowers blown
back by wind – dark center grows

sentry diamond lit at night
two eyes: white birds – white
rose twirled & petals stripped
one by one – arrows like fish

curve down & up – upsidedown
sunflowers – dark center above
umbrella like – long shining blade
gray gloved hand on sword's handle

raises golden lamp as if to kill
yellow lily sprouts up like cobra
arrows rush from shields like hands
to protect – red horizontal bands

paths with even spaces – camera eye
with many irises behind each other
light follows round – crescent moon
with feathers, lady figure smooth

& stars – blue eye behind sweeps
of feathers, two closed eyes: curved
lilies round – arrows, golden, sweep
up left & right, path to bright eye
arrows into center, swirls, water spout

8 15 08

brother's love reassures

white birds fly out of the sun
a plane flies, strings from its wings
flames, arrows follow – it's a green
planet rushing – twirls long length

of light – water reflects, twirls, falls
planet's lower left curve overwhelms
golden hand reaches out – leaves
like flames – flag stripes hold unity

splotches of light, ears of corn, curves
light triangle – gold band circles
arrows fall from grocery bags
along roads & out of pots, narrow truth

each journey has a purpose: to stay
true to one's love: small stars unite
a hand reaches to hold steps to a
house – sunflower with missing petals

a brother's face, sincere, half circle
of sun's light during eclipse, half
golden leaves, half black – his
reassuring voice, deliberate & true

lights race around mountain curves
cars & watches go together
white figure flies upward aslant
the brother's voice taught chess

a giant frog crouched above a pyramid
the light curved around the sunflower,
filled in the missing petals, became
the center of the passing moon, a

creamy light – umbrellas branched
out east & west – a man washes high
windows – jet exhaust, like thousands
of golden arrows, pushes darkness

into blue circular waves – an arrow
straight into sunflower's center
death journey light – petals wave
like fishes, school – her braided

red hair above, face unseen, black
surrounded by, partially covered by
golden fish – petals lashes heart
legs spread eternal love – golden

pyramids fall off her eyes, rush
down – trombones, waterfalls, golden
lily, leaves curve up, green hand
gray-blue eye, golden petals, blood
branch, entirety, planet's wings: fire red

8 21 08

sunflowers then & now

white star upon taking
house, american flag, wind
torso of feeling, youth, softness
fence, tall green stalk – sunflower

female body in gold
white waist belt, petals fall
from dark center – desire excites
youth, cool breeze, shadow over

red cylinder, steps, 3 arrows
stuck in wall, arrows shoot in
& arrows shoot out – golden horns
raised – long-tailed golden fish

move swiftly, hands like forks
up – candles on red rug
big chair with arrows in sheath
beside, white fence next to tree

bed, blanket back, sunset, white
crosses above white lilies, white
tree – he turns his head to hear
"i wanted to be an actress"

the man was gracious & the
tan carpet thick, soft & clean
upsidedown glass, cherish
youthful friendships, cleanliness

golden cross held high with
heart-shaped ring around left
horizontal – house, quiet, with
porch, sunflower big as a win-

dow, against outside window
love, youth, closeness, each a
fidelity – light surrounds in-
terior of square fenced-in

yard, men with horses, darkness
surrounds – reunion true to
what was left at home – true to
seeing remembrance, light &

sunflower horizontal, no cause
church interior – silver wheel
turning, clean & washed heart
love remembrance, love solid, red
petals like butterflies, fire remains

8 23 08

bends head in remembrance

a million lighted candles hold our
hands together – a gold band twirls
our hearts in the blueness – white
windmills & red foxes run the hill-

tops – white tulips & a clothesline
form an entrance into her wings
ferris wheel inside ferris wheel
hand with sparkling diamonds at

finger tips – the long yellow
tulips were pulled sideways & backward
by their stems – the door opens &
no one enters – the door shuts,

white flowers are left – man falls
over the goal post: rodeos & weddings
a boat the size of a pack of matches
floats downstream – white chair in

the blackness – flowers ride a horse
a horse raises its front legs
measure has distance, width &
opening: mauve candles in a

triangle are lit: lamb's fleece
beige leaves hang down & form a circle
a bridge to be measured: green
body with spread arms fronts a door

rabbits march along the baseboard
a stalk of celery, fence, cannon balls
against remembrance – measure
youth by the face's center: joy, loss,

old house with winged creature in
front – eurasian doves, red foxes
by the birch tree – trees & pipes
green prayer hands sprout from a

pot – the birch died above concrete
small fish through tree's branches
wings flutter down by shoes
hands above table's sand

toes with swimming greenery
red female face recedes: warning
white house, hand with propeller ex-
tension, gold triangle, wisp, bends

8 24 08

bees around dark interior

a red rose, slowly rotating, came
up out of the sun – it was
white against the night – such
loss combines friendship & love

quiet voice, steady, over the years
loyal & honest, sunflower tears
the sun fills the sky, yellow
details – trumpets gossip, points

outward, speaks of itself, the one
constant giving – sunflower
returns sideways – burns, yellow
wings spring out like mountains

a table has a shadow, journey has
fear, friendship gathers, holds
arrows rotate, flower retreats
the constant yellow light, flags,

white windmills, longhorn cattle,
parallel rounds, grassy mounds,
doors not locked, friendships remain
many dark centers with yellow petals

arrows dance in mirrored heart
the red rose: keats' death, highway
from mountain to plain, corn & wheat
blackness with eye's sorrow, the in-

tellect hungers for sadness, must
list journey's return to love & death
help's hurt, no books in house, no loss
gracious yellow petals: warmth, window

open, ceaseless talk, conductor,
f.a.a., light, solar, farm, masonry,
arms' journey constantly working
the cow skull orange-red: youth

alive in face's center – white trans-
ference – petals like lilies like arrows
light given off into night – deaths
remembered – rose pink now, rotates

counter-clockwise, slowly, yellow mum
fiery petals reach up, break off
buddha, a hand, a face, journey back
face under sunflower, safe, steady
light strikes path through skull's moon

8 30 08

night before birth

a man makes a fist & puts it down
on a pile of gold coins – an eye
turns sideways – those men
hungry for money turn away

a gold path moves through dark-
ness & curves down – curves &
curves under & holds his hand
white-winged plane above large

blue hand – while men frame
their thoughts with white wings,
wars, hunger, hurricane, loss
never falter – our hands cease

listening – form an apex to
protect a pan catching falling
coins – grasses, fires, buffalo,
golden edges of darkness remain

calm, are encased in breakage
son denies father, unleashes
water, white roses, constant
arrows, burning light all too

many to stop burning frames of
houses – sunflowers & lilacs foam
over waterfalls – pipes, cigarettes
iris, sky, center, far blue, near

death – flames rush around the eye
feathers lift webbed petals, brother
dwells on his own capturings; what
vast pyramid behind the iris

the sun, the holi burning – turn the
light on to kill – one feminine eye
above the spreading blue fan
a hand rotates the royal blue iris

a hypodermic needle fronts the closed
eye – propeller upward, like an
upsidedown table, spins, flames sweep
man walks on burnt-out transient

heart, sparks of light emerge, shine
death, like golden leaves, spring out
death flies, scatters light, lines attach-
ed to sunlight, our sorrow dead, green
rows of arrows, curve, spring, red night

9 1 08

brother's harmony

the white skeleton of a fish,
a flashlight & a sideways tree
form a golden circle – the brightness
& repetition hold weapons at perimeter

keep the human between the warmth
of beasts – the golden arrows deny
ration, lean back, shoot up past the
red horizontal paths – disced fields

the intricate squares of sun's center
the flames at its edges constantly
breaking off, white arrows, moon's
light on river – desire for family

unity, harmony, dead light at bottom's
rest, black narrow – little buttercups
off birth's waning – surfer shoots
down forty-feet high wave – red train

into darkness – golden megaphone
the golden figure a cross, its head
has red electric lines jutting out
under the crown – rays of the sun

the figure: brother, musician,
actor, dead father, silver feather,
green leaf, tall tree, black train
over snow – thick, leafy tree

branches overhanging newly
formed snow – eye, large & snow &
frost around it – flower: rose,
lilacs, tall rushes in lake's center

arrows, like gunfighter's two
guns, shoot light & fury, golden
eyelashes curl up & down, eye
with up-curling golden fish

surrounding it – dark eye large
golden arrows shoot into its centers
rushing golden path down sweeps
golden arrows shoot left & right

the dark sunflower's center
has a golden path round it: marriage,
golden path upward: home, american
flag, blood, deceit, death, golden
hand upward through its stripes, spins gold

9 3 08

Fire Bones

9-4-08 to 1-25-09

Fire Bones

moon & winds

moon seen between white tree's
forked branches – opal curve
glows – "you could power america
with the western nebraska winds"

9 4 08

shadows silenced: talk back

the world has a circle of white
arrows around it – lightning
bolts thrown down the field –
a woman views plankton through

a microscope, later protects urban
plants, animals, birds, on a hilltop
overlooking a famous surfing spot
she takes buses to colleges to teach

two eyes move amidst bands of
white & black, daffodils spring up
light, like a train, rushes, its
engine on fire – the flower on fire

buttercups, green bushes with spiky
tips, dirt paths, nothing obvious –
mint-green water about to spill
over champagne-tinted dam

sail catches bloom – sails like
sunflower petals in breeze, young
boys lift jackets with arms back-
wards & skate surfaces home

shadows on stone, single revolv-
ing arrows spin far from desert
golden flower lifted: green arrows
in red sheath – red & yellow paths

curve down – relentless growing
up, our nation, our asking, arrows
fill the sky – arrows always golden,
our necessary heaven: hope,

death, regeneration – white
arrows, black center, cylinder
twirls – one large yellow tulip
surrenders – mint-green arrows

shoot out, fizzle like fourth of
july snakes – arrows shoot into
planet's curve as sunlight hits
eastern side – snails fall down

interior, wooden curve – sunflowers,
arrows shoot up, sun, swimmers
dive off into blue-green waters
one golden flower rises into
darkness, silo, rowers, gold legs move
around sun, arrows curve down waters

9 10 08

early morning news

white cloud: woman, with her left
hand, holds white towel to cover her
breast, the back of her right hand
touches her forehead

white calla lily in mint-green vase
her open hand
nude, she sits in shadow

white jets' paths upward: cres-
cent moon, mist surrounds it: rain
fire down a mountain in the shape
of a leg with bent knee

bone twirls horizontally in space
like a space station, a listening
device – fires erupt out of a
giant frog's mouth, like the

top of a mountain erupting
tall stack of bananas carried by
black woman on top of her head
white-golden hand, like a fire,

reaches for a city below moun-
tains – passages marked with
sounds of water pouring: white
cross, tall in darkness, shines

mountain with snow resembles
white-headed eagle – sunflower
downward with petals like wings

sunflower in sun, petals upward
like bees – sunflowers in wind
like ladies with hair blown
back – glorious gold in blueness

jets shoot up out of sunflowers
night comes, petals close toward
center – white arrows fall
into large glass – form necklace

white birds in dark blue sky
long white path upward to white
turning circle – crescent moon
clouds shaped like white serpent
door opens: woman walks out

9 12 08

green leaves' dam

the white river snakes down the
mountain – "take deep breaths,
eat crackers & drink 7up"
white tree, white hand reaches

upward – white crown in night
amarillo, san gabriel, denver,
mountain home, hastings, s.o.d.,
manzanola, s.o.d., sidney, s.o.d.,

atwater, sidney – door handle
turning, car wheels: igloos, turkey
huts, sugar beets, wheat & corn
& now, white windmills – western

nebraska winds & american flags
crown: sunflower in the wind
the women & children stood on their
door steps & watched the tornado

everything was quiet; later that
summer were cloudbursts: rain,
getting soaked, then sun & clear sky
golden arm goes up into night stars

sun sparks down, wheat & corn
grow – sun like an old windmill
turns slowly white angel constant
wings long & upturned in fall

arrows move up right & up left
in long cylinder: silo silo
flower, at farm's center, blooms
memory – lights from cars pro-

long harvest day – "i lived 17
places by the time i was 17"
the sunflower's constant draw
& pull – white wings, long narrow

cylinder, awakening blueness
the river snakes down the mountain
like a necklace – yellow flowers in
his hand – light at top, darkness, fall

golden circles, white sheets on clothes-
line, golden petals, white wings –
home, road, family, fields, rivers,
sweeps up to hold darknesses' water

9 13 08

weather vane: crossed arrows

an hourglass spins – top half
one way, bottom the other
the reasons are many & have to do
with friendship & baseball

we sit on the top deck & look down
at the field, & look out at the
mountains – though friendly, we
have to pay attention to the game,

it's not tv, with replays – the blue-
gray river runs along & has a full
moon in the middle – a white
female figure flies – she plays

a violin – she arises from a sun-
flower's center, its arrows acting
as a fence – disclose, eyes above
a fiery wall – cat walks through

sunflower – man stands on the
milky way, does a back flip, green
surfboard vertical, sunflower
large as the moon, moon beside it

ship with many sails in the blue
manifest desire, white figure flies
one way, red flame jets opposite
a crown, a leaf, the sunflower like

the sun only brown center, light
at edges, three arrows shot into
center – sorrow, a woman's face
bent, golden blazing sunflower

must fields possess home, journey?
must light be sole possibility at last?
what darkness lost, ship at sea, arrows
rage, large hand reaches shore, pulls

up, the golden petals swirl inward
like a twirling cup – white horse,
with uplifting mane, runs – golden
water pours out of the sunflower

white horse jumps, sunflower beside
it – bow bent – white arrows shot
into sky – empty void, golden petals
surround, white arrows, white oars

9 15 08

solace remembered

man walks by trailer, waves hit
shore – blue half-circles, quiet
ocean, light sparkles – long light
path like a candle – gold half-circle

man walks on cliff top, arrows
move left, arrows circle right
moon-lit path on ocean, sun spots
flare like a fan – he only knows

apples – man holds flowers, he spins
them – white figure flies through
trees – flies against blue half-
circles – spreads wings – circle of

light on white cashmere coat
peach half with seed – green
reverberations outward – arrows
shot down a shaft of light

three large sunflowers in front
of a bike rack – feathers out of
dark center – calla lily with blue
stamen – large gold hand with

blue ring spinning around finger
sunflower, like spider web crack,
in center of door's glass – red
sash around book: desire,

solace, remembrance, once love
arrows stuck in tree: shelter
petals lift, black horses pull wagon
wings shelter golden ball

green wings open – arrows shoot
each walk, walks uncover long
lengths, golden & unheralded,
workman like – arrows rush

round like racing cars fronting an
american flag – large wall of a
car wash, wordsworth's golden
flowers – sheath of arrows stuck

in tree, american flag, glorious
sun, thin bare tree in light
prairie, sod house, dark sky, light
climbs atop, white winged bird flies

9 16 08

before sleep

eagle's eye, asian woman's eye
behind a spread fan – peacock
tail hides mystery – bless you, muse,
the lava down the mountain

small lizard inside golden leaf

9 16 08

fire bones

ring of fire like shark's teeth
center brightness, solar, search
for solace – family was once
central, our hearts belong to seek-

ing – find sorrow, find reason
white jet plane climbs in blue-
ness – flames make whiteness:
this home: wife, cats, son connected

in voice & spirit – helicopter above
reminds us where we live: she
teaches, i haunt movie houses
brightness in darkness, bewilder-

ing sorrow lost in projected light
& shadow – body made white from
jet's exhaust – one friend in
cedars has not awakened from

anesthesia; one friend came
home yesterday after one week
in cedars & three weeks in rehab:
alcoholism; one friend lost his job

teaching poetry in a magnet school,
after twenty-eight years;
bless my wife for her teaching;
bless emotion; bless first family

lost when the mother died: the
family disassembled; bless
egotism, hunger, all material
greed, all distance, all homes

bless this singular home, brown
sofa, fan on in east hollywood,
night time, pizza for supper, too
much tv, just right movies &

baseball – our hearts' journeys
have brought us to mariposa,
just south of fountain, in little
armenia, next to thai town, north

of korea town – over thirty years
together: peach blossoms in the
rain, top deck at chavez ravine,
nebraska: golden-spined lizard

9 19 08

skins

the sun wore arrows, & suddenly
we were at war – waterfall &
prisms

the white bird has to be a fork,
resurrecting lost kindness, backs up

white flames, fragments caught on
dead branches – porcupines of light

9 21 08

golden belt around her waist

rain on the many-colored pebbles
necklace of white stars – large
golden arrow – the men carried
wood above their heads

green meadow the size of a football
field – white wings around it
indians, with arms full of arrows,
ride horses through golden light

violet flowers surround a slide
nest, golden arrows, one white
leaf floats – branches wings
hours – hearts clean, journey up

to & around sun, a golden wall
woman wears white bikini, window,
lightning like a hand, glasses
moon crescents around sun

raises hammer, distinguishes
love, no cruelty, nor teeth bared
light, like fire burning on fin-
ger's top, lamp to find darkest

light, tiger barely seen – white
moon surrounds apollo, wheel
turns – breast rests – tiger's face
upside down, resolute & still

arrows faintly seen in its turn-
ing – loss from cruelty in spirit
not flesh – journey ahead
golden boat, arrow exhaust

returns, weds, nods, kneels, lost
humility, sun moves away in glory
the first day of autumn, waits
golden flames fluted darkly

dark train & dark necklace, statue
of liberty black-green above the
burning – planes, like knives, fly
up in congress – golden arrows,

horses & wagons over plains, flames
circle above green meadow, heart
lost, golden path, light shines from
above, green arrows rush around planet
jade necklace pulled around her neck

9 22 08

white arrows surround center

long black ditch
where once was a white body with
white arms – arms wrapping a
mint-green box – tulip, like horn

lifted, arrogance, lostness, forlorn
money – white leaves of money
anxious seeds, curving road
like serpent's tail

wind blows back green-leaved
tree sideways – sunflower &
white stars reclaim lostness
light rushes out of sunflower

with such force, sunflower falls
back – white planet with arrows
stuck into it in blackness
white planes jet upward aslant

right – deny, give, steal, remember
the room where we slept in two
single beds separated by a
small night table, opposite a

desk, where i studied, memorized,
next to a closet where our ironed
shirts & pants hung, a .22 rifle
in the corner, memory & smell of

electric trains & tracks & trans-
formers under the bed – window
outward to rectangular, cinder block
apartment buildings, 4 units each

art aleman & i played catch at
4:30 when he came home from work
o brother of lost childhood, you
loaned me your 1950 mercury to

take a girl to the junior prom, i
stole & pawned your rifle to buy
a 1931 ford, drove it a week, you
asked what happened to your rifle

i sold the car for $25, retrieved
the .22 rifle – you live in raleigh,
n.c., i live in east hollywood, ca.
you're recovering from heart

surgery – i go to movies, root for
the dodgers – the white lights
among night's stars cross each
other – white eagle flies toward

my forehead – white windmills
& graves ahead, fences, steers,
boxcars with coal, roads home
fishers hill, viaduct, sod house,

country school, star market,
stag tavern, greenwood cemetery
where our parents' graves are –
we stand in a half-circle,

our sister speaks
train & whistle, circle, arrows
at rest

10 7 08

zeus in a hurry: eye within leaves

distant face, lips, curly hair
discernible, kindness interior – hand
like a tree, curved lines go back
& forth like a clock's bell – where

youth has rushed downward, pulled
tight, knotted itself – ringed fire
green leaves lost at sun's edges

these words are gourds for buddha
arrows rushing over the waterfall
a golden ring with a nail driven
through – her footsteps in the night

little fires at the edge of a glacier
blue mourning: crown of wide, fresh
waterfalls – white lights like fast
boats across the blue – blue, white

& red medals hang down from the
waterfalls' top – like one great
arrow, a giant guitar – stars of
medals at bottom – kingdom of

surfers & small planes zip up
& down – golden daffodils on a
hill, with light shining down

arrows shoot down & form a flower
dripping with ice: no rent, no money,
no kindness, no envy, no dishonor

arrows reign down like chandelier's
light, a plane curves upward, a
golden cross held & raised – one
long, golden arrow, golden fingers

curve down – white waters
rush down, lift & carry flowers
one large sunflower in center
of waterfalls – golden tulips,

golden roses on a hill, freshly
washed, like youth, like kindness:
two hands meet, the bow string
pulled back, arrow between
fingers, string & arrow released
circles the globe like racing
cars, flashes of light, our arms

10 10 08

whale juxtaposed with golden light

the white waves hit the blue
shore: notorious, sadness, no
solace – white footprint, white
flag – an upsidedown arrow like

a tree from heaven: conspicu-
ous – glass turned sideways
white flame turns golden

simple stones, hour glass with
red flash behind it – black bear
walks on golden bolt ledge

white spider, crouched, transforms
into a sunflower, perimeter light
haunts home, lifts barbed wire
slips under, he hides from the guard

by lying in a furrow, wolf,
arrows shot into pumpkin, the
light passes over him – golden
vertical scroll – blackberry

bushes on each side of the path
golden fan with trumpet, elevator
breaks in half, lightning, bare
dry branches: humility, hand &

circle, fallen, green waters sweep
up – light appears slowly like a
sideways pyramid, gray-blue hat
long white candles, lilacs spill

two golden figures & one
far off – white bird flies straight
one dark eye, two dark eyes, she
appears behind peacock tail spread

tree uprooted, fast, golden fish like
canoe: earth curve, harvester,
arrows, feathers, daffodils, golden
exhaust – sunflower's perimeter

broken by darkness: nest, red
horizontal electric light, like a train,
steady, strong, below blue viaduct
it moves across the horizon into
the grove of dark trees: train
into mountain shape: dusk, youth

10 17 08

friendships in market

green banana leaves with
sun shining behind them
white arrows circling, indian
headdress: white feathers

white figure, head first, falls
down in white hail: whiteness
betrays itself to find grace, to
dispel fellow's anger – sun-

flower falls back with arrows
stuck in its center: feathers form
golden cross: four crescent moons
encircle darkness – fires up path

hands upraised about pumpkins
small fires, sunflower petals
surround her eye, precious
banality, kind desire, heart solace

dichotomy, duality, firmness
coal bin, winter wheat, rocks, rusted
car frames, one tree, windmill
circular water tank, yellow leaves

longhorn steers move past golden
circle – sunflower, lion's face,
wings surpass dark center's
fury – white wings above fighters'

planes: turns with hope, small
golden planes fly through perim-
eter's petals – path widens
white leaves against dark sax-

ophones – arrows into sheaths
jewish man from texas, jewish
couple from england, italian
man from providence offer

solace, reason, laughter, shade
arrows released backwards
relief: one violet flower, thin,
fragile, offering shade from sun

sunflower, like klieg light, turns
upward – listening, a comfort
sturdiness in deed, mystery a
kindness – morning friends shade

10 18 08

black vertebrae encased in golden light

white sail, golden dancing figure
circle of fire, white bird above
the circle held, shaken like a
tambourine, starfish, pair of

glasses – royal blue water
flames remain, will not be shaken
out, an edge like snowy moun-
tain peak, yellow flowers burst

from circle's top – white mice
crawl crescent's ridge, golden
arrows in sheath – large light
bulb – hand reaches for it

yellow feathers at arrows' ends
large yellow moon – hands blaze
piano keys – bridge high above
cars – circle's gas jets – flames

into bird, flames rush out like
curved fingernails – rifles
raised above sunflowers, soldiers
in their brown uniforms, lined up

hand raised: stem of sunflower
flames, petals, rush over top
swirl, wind blows smoke back
on rushing engine, circular,

spinning wires, white smoke,
hand, fork, sunflower with two
birds, crossing wings, above top
petals, feathers curve, float down

white arrows plunge down waterfall
hit bottom, straighten out, continue
waters fall, great width, chorus
girls' legs – dancing, arrows cross

arrows, like olympic swimmers, hit
wall, turn, race – arrows fly up,
leave long pyramid-shaped exhaust
thousands of golden arrows shot

downward, hit water, rush eastward
large house like a castle with opera
seats & fountains, white female nudes
swim down sides of inside pool, home
red fires atop walls, arrows, vertebrae

10 22 08

heart no longer lost

lavender & icy sky – the hands
flew upwards – he felt he had
betrayed the source – the
hands came from a renowned

jewish poet's poem in an ele-
vator: the hands flew up from
the book – he spoke incautiously
to an old actor friend, later

felt he had betrayed the source
white winged plane with actual
bird wings that moved like
zephyrs & thousands of white

fish – it was cool in the valley
he reached below the sunflower
& held the stem, broke it,
brown canyon depth beneath

like great receivers, giant
sunflower tilted, yellow perim-
eters blushed, turned, tucked,
white wings followed, niceties

umbrella, closed, held horizontally
circles of arrows – sprouts out-
ward – he turned away from the
killing – arrows gloriously went

upward toward the sun, small
trees, the size of cemetery crosses,
fell, fire behind the forest tempts
arrows crosses sunflowers friends

no reason, just openness, just here
have what's smoke from flower
harvest sun shadows train hope
flower, shield like fan, half-opened

arrows shoot up like planes – black
masts of ships, renewal, seeking
home, lostness, return, shame
mine alone for often aloneness

decides who gains: friendship
an occasion, rest, solace, forgetful-
ness shared – spoken memory, honor
incarnation, rest aloneness, respect
face, shining light, electric red path

10 29 08

golden lamps around the tips

a silver star pressed in at its
sides – white dog – propeller
of small plane turns – the neck-
lace she wore had a red star

at its bottom, soothe, waterfalls
in all directions facing in –
a circle of silver, barbed wire,
wreath, an eye, sunflower

leaf, bone, waterfalls renown
golden arrow & red slippers
saxophone down the waterfall
yellow leaf waves – ferris wheel,

like sunflower on its side, stuck
full of arrows – the changing
emotions keep us together, we
know not the strangeness nor

unkept sorrow, nor newness,
stories told survive anger, sorrow
the turning circles form crescents
pumpkins & gourds before buddha

large red sail, golden feathers
on arrows – white shrouded bird
figure – rose emerges, disfigured
water pours into its center, pushes

arrows aside – fire around sun-
flower's perimeter – bolt of
gold revolving, long length
long ice particles pass above eye

eye, space, void, darkness, above,
to the side – water falls, arrows
embedded around eye – eye nourish-
es, thin lines of water falling

water sweeps down & up – white
then blue, small boats move down –
her lower body opens, darkness
between waters, she lies north

& south, black road, golden eye
wide waterfalls, eyelashes, laven-
der streak upward, blue figure
moves up, sheltered, golden lamps

11 4 08

fingers open eyelid's heart

the long white road turns into
a circle, bewilders an eye,
shelters lostness, wakedness,
an eye straight as a snow cliff

winged & golden topness, glorious
& moon crescent-like, with
chrysanthemum softness, home
i lived that far away once

flames outward, profile: indian
head – the eye, dark & large
burning trail atop, feathers aflame
crescent bottom gold – blueness

with hand pulling back string
& arrow: refrain – revolving cir-
cles like ferris wheels, peach –
seed exposed – arrows rush

outward like waters hitting
shore, solemn & cleansing
surfers off the top of mountain-
ous wave – arrows outward from

above the eye – three slant down
from its center – castle with blue
lamps burning, isolated but connect-
ed by depth – serene blue roundness

hourglass: light shines from its
center – wings fly, golden beetle
solace: pyramid, metallic gray,
silver light inside, sunflower eye

held by hand, an offering, water
falls down, encircle around eye
vertical then horizontal shelter
golden sparks from eye's perimeter

brown, densely, seeded center, tilts
sideways, suddenly golden & sun-
like, quiet again, arrows as eye-
lashes, lava hot again, sultry

wakeful, raging, whole eye golden
fire, a river enclosed, radiant moon
within: pale gray-blue, austere
fingers open vulva, pulsating goldness

11 7 08

Circles Where The Waters Meet

arrows' yellow bonnet

the ocean washes up on the shore
white birds fly – a woman's
mouth opens – morning arrives
white flower on long green stem

large sunflower center with
small yellow petals – green
petals blown sideways in night

indian headdress, long yellow
forearm & hand, yellow wings,
arrows shot into sunflower,
sad heart, industrious nation

her dress bands of color: purple,
yellow, brown, like a bonnet
white stetson – face like a
burning sunflower, old cowboy

curved golden petals like a
crown – arrows' fury, accept-
ance – water pouring, nation
old, firm, flawed, changing light

blood, cross, arrows, boats, deaths
shamed glory – one large silver
arrow goes upward, deep into
blackness – sunflower a large

drum of deer hide – stretched
to make the plains barren of
trees, funnel of wind, o mighty
deaths: sunflower with arrows

stuck in heart, surrounded by
rainbow, console, lead, reclaim
the vertical eye, with silver
arrow leading out – golden light

shines aslant on rocky mountain
black planet with thinning trees
yellow hand emerges, holds sun-
flower, o mighty arrows out

large eye: planet, sunflower, with
homes surrounding, an intricacy
golden center, golden path, washing
vibrating sunlit perimeter mourning

11 13 08

circles where the waters meet

white bird flies between two
blue windows
golden belt across the sky
train with white top moves

cross the horizon – scissors
large like a sky full of black-
birds – white birds swim fast
white plane flaps its wings like

a bird – waters white between
two docked ships – yellow um-
brella-like figure flies, opening
& closing its umbrella – cup of

coffee – white caps hit shore,
yellow butterfly above cliff
sunflower with sunlight on
its petals – swimmers, planes

two white circles – parachute
opens – golden crown in blueness
her leg lifted & bent at the knee
black grapes, symphonies shine

crown, golden road aslant, dark
trees slanted above – lilacs shoot
out like fireworks – hand behind,
an offering – fire behind build-

ing, morning like fire, glorious
blue-white waterfalls, great
width – golden road, a great circle
where names numinous reside,

rise & fall, table with three apple
pies ready for oven – lines with
one golden figure between, a
benediction to silence, waters

wash our feet, arrows fly up like
yellow irises, figures fall back
like falling lamps, straight
the hood of her gown, golden-red

golden line across horizon like
a train, red above, home here
the land golden-red, dark sides
waterfalls clean & blue, far within

11 14 08

golden arrows, eye, bull

red bull with silver horns
twirling like a majorette's baton,
propeller – faith seldom chosen,
breath lost, gained – white planes

jet upward, nation ready, alert
wheels turn – yellow & blue slashes
sunflower & golden road, petals
full like a bush – fury in wind

petals wet with light, eye tipped
thick like a tire, melody with fur,
anxious resolve – star, banana,
white leaves – golden moon behind

arrows move forward, great length
zigzag beneath crown, resolute heart
turning thick silver wheel –
long-horned cattle rush forward

territory, wide waterfalls, eye
with golden arrows circling
arrows, like petals, shoot out
at sunflower's edge – eye sur-

rounded by gold & peacock feathers
cherish the long arrows curving
around her, her heart our warmth
though memory only within night

waterfalls purely white like a
turning tree with no leaves
the legs fall & disappear into
dark water – swimmers swim

between the two down flowing cliffs
golden-white sunflower at bottom
of falls, secure, not sad, not sudden,
arms' rapture, trees begin, rocks

like after rain, wholesome, shiny
land with golden light, like a path,
moves side to side, green hill
crescent moon, black panther

white waters, black-shaped cali-
fornia, separate, white waters,
gates open – hand like a cactus,
twirling white figure into blue

11 15 08

santa ana winds like oceans

a woman waters flowers
flowers, blue, white & pink, the
shape of a cross – a man drives
his car through a valley

golden robe doubled up by itself
white hands about her head
flowers perimeter
white flowers surround one sun-

flower – fires rage incessantly
& the men talk movies
winds cross white road
sun shines strongly between

tree stripped – arrows go round
fire in the house, north, south,
east, crosses freeways, petals
tears, dry – important documents

dogs bark in the neighborhood
helicopters drop water, flame
retardant – fires burn up like
sunflowers, rage for ten miles

five places outside the city
immensity of a blazing house, chino
hills, yorba linda, corona, sylmar,   ·
anaheim hills – the sun shines

at night – white flowers bloom
on a hill – covered wagons, bare
branches, solace, dogs, winds, bones
important documents, smoke on a

hill – white water shot sideways
roads, fire engines, ruddy faces,
strength, endurance, recovery
& the sunflower grows bigger

our arms cannot hold the sorrow
& destruction – solitary walks
in coolness outside holding heat
white with heat like the inside

of a nearly-ripe peach, rhythms
& seeds, embers newly hatched, strewn
3, 4 miles – bright yellow petals, dark
center, sirens three, desert winds

11 15 08

need has meaning

short red lights radiate out
of the arm – the indian wears
one yellow feather in his hair

an upsidedown sunflower
like an umbrella – fire rages
in a fury round the flower

hand, white, reaches up – religion,
corn on the cob – reality changes,
man goes to where he has a need
to go – he arrives, sits, talks, his

friends age – they talk about films
they've seen: "doubt," "milk,"
"defiance," "the earrings of madame de,"
"rachel getting married," the new

james bond film; they talk about
broadway plays; they discuss their
health, the possibility of s.a.g. going
out on strike – a key light is out

the sunflower tilts like a giant
receptor – thanksgiving nears
the milky way is made up of thou-
sands of sunflowers, lending

a yellow tint to the far blueness
birds sink their claws around
branches – feathers fall back
out of sunflowers' perimeters

money lost, war deaths, morality
questioned, stores close – sun-
flowers' centers fall back

two white round horizontal poles
white rays shine down, golden
path – the brother goes to where
he has a need to go – where lost

has gained, has hidden, has chosen
gold floats in blue – our hands
are not tied, goodness has motion

instant now present – golden
hand surfaces in blueness – we
take our hats, our milk, our arms
encircle family, friends

11 25 08

above the blue mountain

the long-handled white hammer
reflects bricks across the water
feet, dozens in a row, step above
graciousness lost, each comic, car

salesman, ad guy, hair dresser,
accountant, returns, resells, wants,
demands to be only his story, his
recognition – white winged filled

with arrows downward – it rains,
each & only each lost for wanting
the whole notion of diamonds
exploding, yellow rays stream out

loyal beast beside master in rain
witness bespoke bewilderment
not delicious, family & work all
story, solace, witness, heal, deny

kingdom his, kingdom hers, service
devout – our hearts are within
our hearts long for more than
money, more than affluence, more

than isolated present, than re-
gional ego, our forefathers work-
ed to frame, to balance, protect –
to give & listen – hear the rain

what was burnt was lost, what our
hearts are looking for: dust, water
against rocks, recognition past one's
present heart: dead solace, water

drops at edges of long flames long
burnt out – to be foolish, careless,
cliffs with windows, souls with
shadows, arrows' long journeys

stars like planes upon the morning
shore – wings above the upsidedown
planet, green & blue – hearts not
set against each competition, each

american hunger for materialism,
for each heart has abundance, gold-
winged beetle with one white eye
drills through, spreads wide, golden scythe

11 26 08

fires from horses & arrows shooting

buffalo, fish, coat hanger,
ornaments on america's tree
arc across the blue sky, white stars
when winter becomes soon

kingdom, years, niceties, shelter
brotherhood ceased – honesty
sold for money – to relocate
heirlooms – silver wreath against

brightness – golden hoops horizontal
then vertical, boxcar, fire wings
golden sticks in bundles, water
flows like arrows through hoops

steeple horizontal – golden fire
around – wings swoop & lift, door,
golden fish like an eye, windless
light above & beyond – arrow cuts

eye in half, strength redeems,
provides turtle, golden, with wings
children follow golden arc: eye
covered with downward sparks

children, strength, country, solace
small black bodies with wings, length
like locomotive – half black, half
brown, with golden horn, silver

circles, like a tunnel, roll
light bulbs of speed, race eter-
nal, our hearts soldered like
wide waterfalls, like fields of

yellow daffodils, schoolyard, soccer,
fence, near silo & train tracks
golden wheat blowing in eagle's
darkness; river, trees, light shines

half heaven, half earth: whale's
tail seen above descent: covered
wagon, ship with smoke, ship with
sails, no wind: arrival, long spears

many men on horses, water wall again
like boats & arrows resurfacing
breath clean, august, all falls con-
verge at center: rescue upturned
arrows: headdress against silver sun

12 5 08

sunflower's concentric circle: escapes

white bird flies from its nest
above the city's white lights
our remains are just – the theft
was slightly wrong, paid in cash

golden circle above golden circle
the men congregated to share
work stories, to laugh, to remain
known as they age in a young

city, young country – the golden
circle was simply hands holding
hands letting go, darkness
commingling with occasional

repetition – like a golden crab:
nebula – a recognition to rely
upon sameness, to listen, to push
back anonymity – birds white

like fire, unite the planet's
perimeter: eclipse, the only ones
in the room save for the servers
waters rain down like arrows

over the falls – sunflower rises
out of the sea, like a sun, a
body worn brown from lusted
life, rolls up, arrows face down

in rows on both sides, to protect
the two topmost leaves coming
together above the road – sun-
flower tilts down like a sun

knife, laser, straight razor of
light across the horizon – men on horses
hold torches, ride the curve – guns
spring quiet above mountain's

shining fire: cross, tree, silence
our names resilient: work, age,
resourceful, loyal; our hearts lost
no longer – the waters flow down,

create cylinder, sun's light at back
end – white bird, like large plane,
flies again – horizontal cross in
blueness, streaks throughout heart

12 9 08

bench, rain, night, sun

lamb, white feather – south of the
pier, a slightly opened door
the circle had a partially white
section: hope, rain coming

three stripes of darkness, speedy
clouds – a white mushroom, large
beneath the circle – was it his
handwriting, the son to father?

prayer hands for those near the
bus station, dooms of shelter, she
would need patience, focus, "are
you ready to come in?" the long

white triangle measures sadness,
hope, nothing like motels, war
over; sunflower brims, ferris
wheel powered by sun, pier's end

star explodes in white light,
plane released, seeks beyond
fires' edges, turns, too old to
stock shelves in a store, a widow

of a poet – she slept on a bench
near the pacific ocean, weathered
face – burning circle with
justice's scales in center, shapes

like heart, twin loss, twin hope
wheat fields shaped vertical &
horizontal – golden feathers
front moon, large sunflower

moves across the sky, like a
planet – green eye (jade
pyramid) – father turns back,
refuses, he was once a soldier

petals long & golden, her eye-
lashes, our forgiveness for our
limitations' lament: sorrow,
white-tipped arrows, like flags

at an angle, like raised bugles,
"are you ready to come in?" gold
fishes move up, sideways, blood &
wind, restless loss opens door,
fiery circle breaks in half, solace

12 24 08

sunflower eye with green wings

hand mirror, four flowers stand
as gates – two golden rockets
shoot past – her eye with golden
wheat eyelashes, a tree made of

wheat stands alone, circles of
golden barbed wire – white
flower darts, wheat waving
circles the corner, wheat flows

down like waterfall – white
flowers a globe, large as a planet
flowers flow close to the ground –
her eye majestic & sensual

serene, golden flowers encircle
dark mystery – fire night, wild
rushes, arrows, trees, fields,
rigors of nights – white flowers

dance until golden, until night
sweeps its shadow – dark eye,
golden wheat fields, trees made
of wheat – two white flowers

shine a path for opening wings,
fragile & thin, green large as
a nation's hymns, white flower
upsidedown like an umbrella, floats

eye behind darkness, blue front
wall, golden eyelashes drape over
thin golden wheels, sharp rush-
ing arrows, thousands of small

fishes, eye like a pearl, high
atop a straight, taut rope,
arrows rush around eye, black-
ness saddens death, gold far off

golden-winged figure swoops down,
has eye like falcon, savage, piercing,
alone – golden wing leaves down-
ward trail – her dress many sweeps

of golden aisles, black square blinks
behind far off gold circle, blue sky,
scarlet lines, thin membranes:
loss, heart, death, birth, golden hands at the blinds

12 30 08

golden cradle

two wings separated
flower deep in the well
half circle moves upward

white-chested cat, hand
surrounds fire, surrenders
leaves outside window, warmth

near, fire ranges, an arrow,
a fence, fire surrounds eye –
wings with upsweep speed

arrows & wings perimeter
golden side of distant ring
measure distance, loss, newness

years, mobility, love has grown
my love sleeps, her hair has a
crown, sea water, birch trees,
lilacs – she hears exiles: red

flowers on golden swans; she
ages: gold & red horizontal spine
green belt through her eyes

far off green diamond surrounded
by trapezoid – red arms, beige
dress, like bird's tail fanned out

sword pulled out of lavender
rose – leaves turn counter-
clockwise, o ancient hands with

splendor & light, rays shine up,
train emerges from center –
golden boat climbs height,
white rose, wings merge, turn

icy arrows shoot downward
golden hand, wrist bent, arm
unseen: hand with light

measure not loss, arrow moves
up, arrow points down, golden
windmills stand on each side

triangle, bell, circle, fence,
road, heart, eye with golden
lashes – hearts secure road
golden, surrounds blackness, grain

1 4 09

saxophone on side like life raft

a key chain, & the water wavers
blue & icy against the rocks
narrow river rages, awake, down-
wards – white sails, green trees

long golden path: narrow horizon
long-eared leaves, like kanga-
roos, skull, yellow, bouquets
flowers stand out from brown

center, empty wheat field, poppies
orange & tall: refrain, distant
sunflower turns red & dances
heart has a home – nourish dis-

tance, upsidedown white flower sweeps
sunshine forces down on bloom
golden light, like a beak, moves
across hilltop – opposite, a razor-

back mammal moves forward –
golden scroll between opulent
sofas, bridge suspension, harp
like lonely sailor's hymn holds

memory, heart honest, waits to say
hello, goodbye, god bless; golden
bullets held by finger & thumb
bullets between bricks – bottom

half of sun's ridges: bright, shiny,
fiery, ragged, red pipe revolves,
water squirts – both sides, under-
neath, red like hell – shovel, spike,

arrows, knives, feather: legacy
forward, connection, saved, mouth,
large lips – claws clamp down
circles of light with bat outside

basement window – bat's wings
spread – light blue sky with pointed
tendrils' lights awakening
arrows fall down into a river of

eggs cooking in milk, boat with
arrows as oars, dark anglos, long-
lighted spear, wharves, dark men
in boats come ashore, sharp golden spear

1 15 09

wings & hand, stars beyond

umbrella, water shoots upward
mountain tops zigzag
crescent moons follow one another
like nights out of sleeves

white dog shaped like a small car
walks, wags its tail proudly
hand of cards spread
front end of large gun like a loco-

motive, figure falling – sky diver
lilacs in a row, like a fence, fold
forward – their feet on the other
side of the fence continue forward

candles around perimeter, unlit,
long & wide golden arrow ready
for release, walks like vaude-
villian, one leg bent & curled

sunflower circles, stems with
white-tipped leaves – hand bones
golden lighted train below horizon
burning candles – wheat field

ladies' legs slipping out of gar-
ments, leaning slightly, long
golden rectangle within blue-
gray moon – scarlet band above

pulses – light green leaves
spill out – dark center:
apple, pale moon, violet
surrounds like scarf – edges

above cut by scissors, inch by
inches – scarlet hand pushes
up dark planet – sunflower,
steel handle glistens, wings up

from horse & rider, waterfalls
left, water rushes up to right
golden arrows – flags unfurled
from individual fingers, arrows

shoot up, each tip a sunflower
bound at bottom center, small razors
white light at mountain's far eastern
top: fire climbs circumference

1 25 09

About the author

HARRY E. NORTHUP has had nine previous books of poetry published: *Amarillo Born, the jon voight poems, Eros Ash, Enough the Great Running Chapel, the images we possess kill the capturing, The Ragged Vertical, Reunions, Greatest Hits, 1966-2001,* and *Red Snow Fence.* He received his B.A. in English from C.S.U.N., where he studied verse with Ann Stanford. New Alliance Records has released his "Personal Crime," new and selected poems from 1966-1991, on CD and cassette audio recording, and "Homes" on CD. Northup has made a living as an actor for over thirty years, acting in thirty-seven films, including "Mean Streets," "Taxi Driver" (1976 Palme d'Or winner at Cannes), "Over the Edge" (starring role), and "The Silence of the Lambs" (1991 Oscar winner for Best Picture). Harry is a member of the Academy of Motion Picture Arts and Sciences. Lewis MacAdams, in the *L.A. Weekly,* wrote, "Northup is the poet laureate of east Hollywood." Harry is married to poet Holly Prado.

Also by Cahuenga Press

Specific Mysteries
by Holly Prado, 1991 (OP)

You and the Night and the Music
by James Cushing, 1991 (OP)

Ordinary Snake Dance
by Phoebe MacAdams, 1994
(no ISBN) $10

The Ragged Vertical
by Harry E. Northup, 1996
(ISBN 978-0-9649240-0-0) $15

Sacrifice
by Cecilia Woloch, 1997
(ISBN 978-0-9649240-4-8) $12

Esperanza: Poems for Orpheus
by Holly Prado, 1998
(ISBN 978-0-9649240-5-5) $12

The Length of an Afternoon
by James Cushing, 1999
(ISBN 978-0-9649240-6-2) $12

Homelands
by Jonathan Cott, 2000
(ISBN 978-0-9649240-7-9) $12

Dreaming the Garden
by Ann Stanford, 2001
(ISBN 978-0-9649240-8-6) $15

Reunions
by Harry E. Northup, 2001
(ISBN 978-0-9649240-9-3) $15

Tsigan
by Cecilia Woloch, 2002
(ISBN 978-0-9715519-0-9) $13

Livelihood
by Phoebe MacAdams, 2003
(ISBN 978-0-9715519-1-6) $12

These Mirrors Prove It
by Holly Prado, 2004
(ISBN 978-0-9715519-3-0) $20

Undercurrent Blues
by James Cushing, 2005
(ISBN 978-0-9715519-4-7) $15

Red Snow Fence
by Harry E. Northup, 2006
(ISBN 978-0-9715519-5-4) $15

Strange Grace
by Phoebe MacAdams, 2007
(ISBN 978-0-9715519-6-1) $15

From One to the Next
by Holly Prado, 2008
(ISBN 978-0-9715519-7-8) $15

Pinocchio's Revolution
by James Cushing, 2009
(ISBN 978-0-9715519-8-5) $15

For each book ordered,
add $5.50 (shipping & handling)
and send to:
Cahuenga Press
1256 North Mariposa Avenue
Los Angeles, CA 90029